香港國際詩歌之夜 *2015*
INTERNATIONAL POETRY NIGHTS IN HONG KONG

編輯 Editors

北島 Bei Dao

陳嘉恩 Shelby K. Y. Chan

方梓勳 Gilbert C. F. Fong

柯夏智 Lucas Klein

馬德松 Christopher Mattison

宋子江 Chris Song

目錄 Contents

彼得·科爾
Peter Cole

Of Time and Intensity

Is Time a dispersion of intensity?
For epiphanists, maybe, but not for me—
for whom Time is a transposition
of immensity into a lower key.

時間與深刻

時間能磨滅深刻嗎?
對頓悟者而言,也許如是吧。
我卻認為,時間最能
把浩瀚化為低調。

(何麗明　譯)

On Being Partial

I'm partial to what's possible,
he thought—not the ineffable,
distant, devoid of insistence
and temperament that tampers,
or tramples
          Not the impersonal,
but that which hovers here
between the "I" of the opening
and the "us" of your possible listening
now, or in the imperfect
tense and tension of what
in fact articulates the eternal
That abstract revelation
and slippery duration
to which, it seems, I'm given
and because of which I'm never
finished with anything, as though living
itself were an endless translation

談偏愛

我對有可能發生的特別偏愛，
他想──不要說不出的，
冷淡無情，易於放棄
及按捺怒氣或蹂躪
性情的
　　　　不要客觀的，
要那徘徊於這裏的，
位於「我」的開端
與「我們」聆聽之間，
或是於未完成
時態與張力中
表達永恆的
抽象的揭示
及含糊的時間
這一切我都擁有
亦正因此我永遠
難於完成任何東西，生活
猶如是永無止境的翻譯

（何麗明　譯）

Song of the Shattering Vessels

Either the world is coming together
or else the world is falling apart—
   here—now—along these letters,
   against the walls of every heart.

Today, tomorrow, within its weather,
the end or beginning's about to start—
   the world impossibly coming together
   or very possibly falling apart.

Now the lovers' mouths are open—
maybe the miracle's about to start:
   the world within us coming together
   because all around us it's falling apart.

Even as they speak, he wonders,
even as the fear departs:
   Is that the world coming together?
   Can they keep it from falling apart?

The image, gradually, is growing sharper;
now the sound is like a dart:
    It seemed their world was coming together,
    but in fact it was falling apart.

That's the nightmare, that's the terror,
that's the Isaac of this art—
    which sees that the world might come together
    if only we're willing to take it apart.

The dream, the lure, isn't an answer
that might be plotted along some chart—
    as we know the world that's coming together
    within our knowing's falling apart.

船隻粉碎之歌

要不這個世界結合
要不這個世界分裂——
　　這裏——現在——字裏行間，
　　刻在每顆心臟的心壁。

今日，明日，普天氣下，
終結，開端，快要開始——
　　世界不可能的結合
　　或是極有可能的分裂。

現在情人的嘴張開——
也許奇蹟將要發生：
　　我們的內心緊緊結合
　　因身外的全在分裂。

在談話之際，他心想，
即使擔憂逐步遠離：
　　世界真的在結合嗎？
　　他們可以讓它不分裂嗎？

畫面，逐漸的，更清晰；
現在聲音猶如飛鏢：
　　他們的世界似結合，
　　事實上它已在分裂。

這是惡夢，這是恐懼，
這是以撒犧牲的故事——
　　世界如果想要結合
　　我們先得願意分裂。

夢想，誘惑，不是答案
可用圖表細心計劃——
　　我們知道世界在結合
　　因為了解了它的分裂。

（何麗明　譯）

The Invention of Influence: An Agon

Part One

*The following considerations are based upon
a single example of the "influencing machine"
complained of by a certain type of schizophrenic patient.*
                    Victor Tausk (Vienna, 1919)

It's a machine, said the doctor,
    of a mystical nature—
reported on at times by patients.
    Their knowledge notwithstanding,
witnesses are able to offer
    only the vaguest of hints
as to how the air loom functions.
    It makes them see pictures. It produces
thoughts and feelings, and also removes them,
    by means of mysterious forces.
It brings about changes within the body—
    sensation and even emission,
a palpable kind of impregnation,
    as one becomes a host.
For some it's driven by faint effluvia

derived from human breath;
for others electric charges are sent
    directly into the brain.
It's born of a need to explain the cause
    of things inherent in man.
Certain factors are always involved:
    Enemies. Displaced erotic
tension. Boundaries are called into question
    as though one's thoughts were "given"
and knowledge implanted from beyond—
    so what's within is known.
One does nothing on one's own.
    Strings are pulled and buttons
pressed, all to evade an anxiety
    that rears its head at the heart
of the void in avoidance. The echoes begin:
    The cure as illness, the illness
as cure. Thus the revolving door
    that becomes a lament for the makers—
and for those who fall prey to the powers—
    of this most intricate machine.

影響之發明：一次競逐

第一部分

以下思考是基於一部「影響機器」
某種精神分裂症的患者曾對此諸多抱怨
域陀·陶斯克（維也納，1919）

醫生說，這是一部機器
　　它有種神秘的性質——
病患常常會說起它。
　　考慮到他們的知識
這些證人只能提供
　　最隱晦的暗示
例如噴氣織機的運作。
　　它讓他們看到圖畫。它能產生
想法和感覺，也有神秘的力量
　　把它們抹去。
它會使身體發生變化——
　　官感，甚至排泄，
一種有觸感的受胎，
　　變成一個宿主。

有人認為，人類呼吸散發的
　　微弱氣味使它運轉起來；
而有人則認為，電荷
　　被直接傳送到腦部。
它產生自一種解釋的需要，
　　解釋人類本質的源起。
某些因素總在作祟：
　　敵人。性的緊張
被錯置。邊界被質疑
　　就像人的想法被「賦予」
別處的知識被植入——
　　所以其中一切皆是已知。
一個人無法獨自完成。
　　繩子拉過了，按鈕
按過了，一切都是為了避免
　　腦後的焦慮，而頭腦
就在避免的空洞的洞。回音來了：
　　療癒即疾病，疾病
即療癒。因此那扇旋轉門
　　變成製造者的哀輓——

還有那些人深受權力錯綜之苦——
　　這部最龐雜的機器。

（宋子江　譯）

From "The Invention of Influence"

We held within us dark forces
(Freud said of a friend he'd miss)
inaccessible to analysis—
that something which is most mysterious
and makes the Jew just what he is.

選自〈影響之發明〉

我們的內心貯藏著黑暗之力
　（想念朋友，弗洛伊德說起）
既無法進入，也無法分析──
它是最神秘的事
把猶太人變成他自己

　（宋子江　譯）

From "The Invention of Influence"

6.

That a son can't bear his name is a shame, or a sham,
like one who's not quite his own man
(a sun with a "u"—to a larger system).
A son with an "O" of address, or an "o"—as before
the "h"—of a sigh, says I am only I in relation.
And yet, sons make a nation.

Sons for some are angels,
for others baubles, or squinting infants,
a kind of endorsement,
or not what was meant. Or a torment.
A grown son referred to as such, it's true,
is often a kind of embarrassment.

One son is said to be God, or God's.
Another's merely a mother's deity.
A son is a link in a chain that links, like a gang's,
or a tutelary. Being a son involves a bond

or being bound. It's a tie that blinds and defines.
That keeps one in line. At times it's like wine,

but then it's a chink in the good old armor.
The favorite son is often a charmer.
A son might marry the farmer's daughter
and have sons or a son's daughters.
Certain sons are marked for slaughter.
Once a son, always a son, even when one is a father.

But sometimes a son is a *door* to the father.
And then that son's seeing is double,
and so he believes that relation is noble
and the sole source of becoming singular
so as to matter, somehow, to others.
Thus a son gives birth to his brothers.

That a son is a name, then, isn't a game,
though it is up for grabs. And that's not a shame,
it's a tradition. A son's an emission.

Desire's expression. A bearer of cues, and clues,
a spooked thing—and maybe an influence, or just a
    fluency,
demanding or dormant, through you, through me.

選自〈影響之發明〉

6.

作為兒子，無法忍受自己的名字，是羞恥，或騙子，

就像一個沒有主見的人

（太陽沒有「、」，變成更大的系統）。

兒子沒有中心的「一」，或沒有從前的「」」

嘆息的「口」，說我只是關聯中的我。

但是一幫兒子能成就一個國族。

兒子，有人覺得是天使

有人覺得是朱義盛，或眯眼的嬰兒

某種授意，

而非原意。又或者熬炙。

這樣一個長大的兒子，真的如此，

常常只是一種失禮。

有一個兒子，說是上帝，或上帝的兒子。

另一個兒子只是一個母親的位格。

兒子是鎖鏈中的鏈，如群體中的相連，

或守護神。作為兒子，意味著羈絆

或被捆綁。這是一條紐帶既蒙眼又立定邊界。

把人定位於行列當中。有時它就像酒，

但它是陳舊而完好的盔甲上的縫隙。
最愛的兒子常常讓人癡迷。
一個兒子或會娶上農家的女兒
再生兒子，或者一個兒子的女兒。
有些兒子被標記成屠宰物。
一日兒子終身兒子，即便兒子已為人父。

但是兒子有時是父親的一扇門。
兒子所看到的都是雙重的，
所以他相信這種關係是高貴的
變成單獨個體的唯一源泉
對事物甚至其餘一切都如此。
因此兒子也生出他的兄弟。

兒子是一個名字，而不是一場遊戲，
雖然它也隨手可得。它不是恥辱，
而是傳統，兒子的驅除，
慾望的表述，暗示或線索的背負，
駭人之事——或只是影響或流暢
苛縛或蟄伏，透過你，透過我。

(宋子江　譯)

Paranoia: A Primer

1.
The paranoid parses all she hears
until it sounds like what she fears;

she fears what's always about to be said,
and so her fear is endlessly fed.

2.
Around her head like a halo it hovers,
a nimbus of hatred of self that smothers

others as well in the smog of its knowing
that knowing is never what's really going

on, and so on, and on it goes—
further and further from what love does.

3.
She ponders the sea of poisonous thoughts
that teach not a thing but *can* be taught.

Within the whirlpool of her mind,
she's caught as Life is left behind—

like a swimmer, swept out to sea on a tide,
which holds that nothing she's had to hide.

4.
A loom loud through the warp of her soul,
set in a room, beyond her control

and behind what anyone said, everywhere—
such were the fruits of her despair:

the choreography of her defense
against the contraptions of Influence,

the strings pulled, as though from afar,
jerking the puppets that we are.

多疑者入門

1.

多疑者剖析她的所聞所見
直至一切可憂慮的都浮現；

她總是擔憂誰將會說甚麼，
她的憂慮也因此恆久得多。

2.

在她頭頂懸浮有如光環，
是那自我厭惡的濃雨雲。

別人也窒息於這煙霧中，
雖然了解情況也不中用。

如此這般沒了沒完──
越是遠離愛的根本。

3.

她估量滿海的有害思想
從中卻甚麼都學不會

在她腦海內的漩渦，
生命似是略她而過——

她像泳兒沖出大海，
甚麼都可袒露汪洋。

4.
隱現的巨響纏繞她歪曲的心靈，
埋藏在一室內，控制不了

背後大家都説，到處可見——
這就是她整天憂慮的結果：

她細心編排她的防守
對抗小玩意兒的影響，

遠處誰在緊拉木偶的線，
我們跌宕猶如懸絲傀儡。

（何麗明　譯）

Improvisation on Lines by Isaac the Blind

Only by sucking, not by knowing,
can the subtle essence be conveyed—
sap of the word and the world's flowing

that raises the scent of the almond blossoming,
and yellows the bulbul in the olive's jade.
Only by sucking, not by knowing.

The grass and oxalis by the pines growing
are luminous in us—petal and blade—
as sap of the word and the world's flowing;

a flicker rising from embers glowing;
light trapped in the tree's sweet braid
of what it was sucking. Not by knowing

is the amber honey of persimmon drawn in.
An anemone piercing the clover persuades me—
sap of the word and the world is flowing

across separation, through wisdom's bestowing,
and in that persuasion choices are made:
But only by sucking, not by knowing
that sap of the word through the world is flowing.

即興創作

唯有透過吸吮，不是認識，
微妙的精髓才能傳遞——
文字與世界的汁液流出

提升綻放中杏樹的芳香，
使橄欖綠的夜鶯變得微黃。
唯有透過吸吮，不是認識。

在青松旁生長的酢漿草及野草
在我們間發亮——花瓣與葉片——
當文字與世界的汁液流出；

小火苗發放閃爍光火；
光隱藏於樹的甜瓣子
所吸吮的。不是認識

那被吸入金黃蜜汁的柿子。
銀蓮花刺穿三葉草說服我——
文字與世界的汁液流出

越過分隔，通過智慧的予贈，
就在這情況下做出決定：
唯有透過吸吮，不是認識
那文字與世界流出的汁液。

（何麗明　譯）

Coexistence:

A Lost and Almost Found Poem

> *And the Levites shall speak, and say*
> *unto all the men of Israel, with a loud voice:*

Over the border the barrier winds,
devouring orchards of various kinds.

Cursed be he that taketh away
* the landmark of his neighbor.*
And all the people shall say, Amen.

The road was blocked in a battle of wills—
as the lame and sightless trudged through the hills.

Cursed be he that maketh the blind
* to go astray in the way.*
And all the people shall say, Amen.

The army has nearly written a poem:
You'll now need a permit just to stay home.

Cursed be he that perverteth the justice
due to the stranger (in Scripture).
And all the people shall say, Amen.

Taken away—in the dead of night—
by the secret policeman, who might be a Levite.

Cursed be he that turneth to smite
his neighbor in secret murder.
And all the people shall say, Amen—

as peace is sought through depredation,
living together in separation.

Cursed be he that confirmeth not
the words of this law—to do them.
And all the people shall say, Amen.

同存：
一首失而幾乎復得的詩

利未人要向
以色列眾人高聲説：

越過邊界障礙重重，
繁種的果園被吞沒。

詛咒那奪去
 鄰人地標的。
眾人道，阿門。

鬥爭中道路被封閉——
跛子瞎子跋涉上山。

詛咒那引致
 盲人迷路的。
眾人道，阿門。

軍隊將完成一詩歌：
留家者要獲得許可。

36

詛咒那以外人為名
　　（經文所示）而毀滅正義的。
眾人道，阿門。

被奪去——夜闌人靜時——
密探可能是利未人。

詛咒那捶打
　　及暗殺鄰人的。
眾人道，阿門——

要和平得先歷破壞，
於分裂間尋求共存。

詛咒那不認同
　　這定律——但奉行的。
眾人道，阿門。

（何麗明　譯）

Israel Is

Israel is he, or she, who wrestles
with God—call him what you will,

not some goon (with a rabbi and gun)
in a pre-fab home on a biblical hill.

以色列是

以色列是他，是她，與神
拚鬥——無論你怎樣稱呼他，

在那之前不是無賴（引述教士或手持武器）
於《聖經》提到的山上建設活動房屋並定居

（何麗明　譯）

Radiant morning funneling blue: into the glow of evening's robes. As though she knew what she wanted to do, or who she'd told. There are, said the kabbalist, two hundred and thirty-one gates in the soul. But did he mean the soul of all—or only Israel? Or maybe the Mind they call Supernal? And gates to what? As doors to where? Make, say the Fathers, a fence for Scripture (of which it's written: "Turn it and turn it, all is in it"). They're making a fence to guard the future...of the People, it says in the paper. And it has many gates as well. And they too are in the soul, and of Israel. But gates to where? Doors for whom? Under the glow of evening's robe. And into the radiant morning blue.

光芒的早上匯聚天藍：光彩一直延伸至晚上的袍子。她好像知道她的心意，或是她告知了誰。據卡巴拉說，心靈共有二百三十一道大門。可是他指的是世間所有的心靈，還是侷限於以色列？還是人們所憧憬的超凡？況且，它們是甚麼樣的大門，通往何處？建造，父親們道，保衛《聖經》的圍牆（上面如此寫道：「轉了又轉，萬事盡在於此」）。他們在建造圍牆保衛未來……保衛人民，它寫在那張紙上。那圍牆也有多道大門。心靈也是如此，以色列亦然。但是，這些大門通往何方，為誰而設？在晚上的袍子的光彩之下。一直延伸至早上匯聚天藍。

（何麗明　譯）

(Valent) Lines for A.

What law and power has blessed me so
that in this provocation of flesh
    I have been wedded to gentleness?

*

Delicacy of an intricate
mesh of our thought and meals and talking
    has brought me to this exaltation

of syllables and a speechlessness—
to December dusk, and desk, and skin
    in the amber of our listening.

*

Dawn again pink with munificence;
heart again blurred by its ignorance:
    toward you in that equation I turn—

and you, in turn, involve our being
spun like wool from which soul is weaving
  a use for that useless opulence.

                    *

Doing and making—the end served by
what it is we make, and what we do,
  is what has made me: making and you.

給A.的（情）詩

甚麼法律及權勢祝福我
使我在這肉體的挑釁間
　　　能對溫柔如此的執著？

　　　　　　＊

我們所思，所吃及所說的
全都微妙的糾纏於一塊
　　　令我感受到

音節的升華及一時的無語——
還有十二月的黃昏，書桌，體膚
　　　在我們互相聆聽間變成永恆。

　　　　　　＊

破曉又至，慷慨的粉紅照亮天際；
我的心也再次被愚昧蒙蔽：
　　　我轉向我們的戀愛程式——

而你，而你，把我們
猶如羊毛一樣紡織，編製心靈
　　給無用的奢華締造一個用途。

　　　　　*

行動與創造——結果取決於
我們創造的及我們的行動，
　　鑄就了今天的我：創造與你。

（何麗明　譯）

From "Notes on Bewilderment"

XLVI.
Lord, goes the prayer, increase my bewilderment,
which really means allow me to question
everything, but not be lost within that
stance to the small flowers of common sense
in season. Increase, Lord, my discontent.

XLVII.
But keep me from resentment. Reason as well
has its season, although we don't believe it,
or put too much faith in it. It's true that
one and one, on occasion, is three or more.
And the middle way *is* often mystical.

XLVIII.
Lord, goes the prayer, keep me from delusion.
Which really means allow my mind to open
to all that comes my way, without bringing
ruin upon me—through fusion of things that are
distinct at heart. Keep me from conclusion.

XLIX.

While the case is being made. And the world
is all that is the case. Keep me from too much
seclusion. Increase my confusion with
Thee, it says. But is that in fact another
matter, I wondered, as the dervishes whirled?

L.

And may my love and language lead me into
that perplexity, and that simplicity,
altering what I might otherwise be.
But let it happen through speech's clarity—
as normal magic, which certain words renew.

選自〈困惑筆記〉

XLVI.

上帝啊，據禱文道，請讓我更為困惑，
換言之請容許我質疑
一切事物，但不要讓我迷失
於普通常識中小花朵之盛放
的季節。增加，上帝啊，我的不滿。

XLVII.

但不要容許我心懷怨恨。理性
也是季候性的，縱然我們不相信，
或是對它太信奉。事實上
一加一，有些時候，等於三或更多。
中庸的真理有時確實是頗神秘的。

XLVIII.

上帝啊，據禱文道，請讓我遠離虛想。
也即是說請准許我的思想開放
能接納一切向我而來的，但不會
把我摧毀——透過融合
緊記於心的事物。別讓我妄下判斷。

XLIX.

我們還在討論這事。這個世界
才是大前提。請不要讓我太愛
孤寂。增加我對上帝您的疑惑。
但，我想，或許那是另一
話題，好像托鉢僧跳回旋舞？

L.

就讓我的愛人與語言引領我
了解茫然，了解簡易，
要不然就把我改造。
讓這一切透過清晰言語發生——
尋常的奇妙，更新某些字詞。

（何麗明　譯）

News That Stays

"It's a multiday process ...
                Under stress,
officially MIA, with a mission. Friendly fire.
   That's not your question?
     I have a good *answer* for it.

Sorry, but we just can't discuss that,
and I can't even discuss why we can't discuss it.

Let me walk you through that decision. Unhindered:

Elite

                Republican

                                Guard.

Cut it off and then kill it. In my mind's eye . . . a thousand
    points of light. If you've
        got a hammer, *find* a nail.

   What the vulnerabilities are.

I'm not trying to
gaff the question. That's a service prerogative.

To classify these folks as prisoners of war.

...

Could you tell us, Pete, if the slick will spread
    and poison all the waters in the region? I
    don't think we have a good feeling for that.

Something has happened to his country
    that he doesn't want us to see.

A daisy cutter, to soften-up the troops.
Just ripple off . . . into infinity!
    A new order. Tel Aviv . . . a
crematorium. We haven't yet reached, I think,
        a point of diminishing

returns. By popular demand. Mr. Ambassador,
thank you very much for your time. My pleasure."

—*The Gulf War, 1991*

逗留的新聞

「那過程長達數天……
　　　　　　在壓力下
他放棄任務。誤傷隊友。
　那不是你問的問題？
　　　但我可以提供一個好的答案。

抱歉，但我們實在不能談論那事，
也不能談論我們為何不能談論那事。

讓我告訴你那決定是如何通過的。毫無保留的：

精銳

　　　　　　　共和國

　　　　　　　　　　　　　衛隊。

把它剪斷，然後殺掉。在我眼裏……千
　點光凝聚。
　　　　若你擁有一個錘子，就應找到那枚釘子。

了解他方的弱點。

我並無意
迴避你的問題。那是服務的特權。

把他們標為戰俘。

　　　　　……

請告訴我們，彼得，石油會否覆蓋
　　及毒化所有沿海區域？我們
　　對這事很不是味兒。

他的國家發生了事
　　但他不想我們目睹。

投射滾球，削弱對方的軍隊。
像漣漪般擴散……無盡無窮！
　　新秩序。特拉維夫……
火葬場。我們還未到達
　　　　收益遞減

的地步。徇眾要求。大使先生，
很感謝你的時間。這是我的榮幸。」

——波斯灣戰爭，1991

（何麗明　譯）

54

彼得·科爾，最近發表的詩集為《影響的發明》(2014)，譯作包括《卡巴拉詩歌：猶太傳統的神秘詩歌》(2012)、《詩之夢：西班牙的希伯來文詩歌(950–1492)》(2007)，以及阿赫朗·沙布泰、塔哈·穆罕穆德·阿里、尤爾·霍夫曼等人的文學作品。科爾曾獲「國家藝術獎金」、「古根漢基金會獎」、「國家猶太圖書獎（詩歌類）」、「筆會翻譯獎（詩歌類）」、「美國藝文學會文學獎」、「麥克阿瑟獎」等。科爾常年往返於耶路撒冷和美國康納狄克州紐黑文城。

Peter Cole's most recent book of poems is *The Invention of Influence* (New Directions, 2014). His many volumes of translation include *The Poetry of Kabbalah: Mystical Verse from the Jewish Tradition* (Yale, 2012) and *The Dream of the Poem: Hebrew Poetry from Muslim and Christian Spain, 950–1492* (Princeton, 2007), as well as poetry and fiction by Aharon Shabtai, Taha Muhammad Ali, Yoel Hoffmann, and others. Cole has received numerous honors for his work, including fellowships from the National Endowment for the Arts and the Guggenheim Foundation, the National Jewish Book Award for Poetry, the PEN Translation Award for Poetry, and an Award in Literature from the American Academy of Arts and Letters. He was named a MacArthur Fellow in 2007. He divides his time between Jerusalem and New Haven, Connecticut.

出版 Publisher
香港中文大學出版社 The Chinese University Press

封面影像 Cover Image
北島 Bei Dao

出版日期 Date of Publication
二零一五年十一月 November 2015

國際書號 ISBN
978- 962- 996- 736- 9

香港國際詩歌之夜 2015 International Poetry Nights in Hong Kong 2015
主辦單位 Organizer
香港中文大學文學院 Faculty of Arts, The Chinese University of Hong Kong

協辦單位 Co-organizers
香港中文大學中國文化研究所
Institute of Chinese Studies, The Chinese University of Hong Kong
香港中文大學出版社 The Chinese University Press
香港兆基創意書院 HKICC Lee Shau Kee School of Creativity
廣州時刻文化傳播有限公司 Moment Communications

贊助 Sponsors
香港法國文化協會 Alliance Française de Hong Kong
上海廿一文化發展有限公司 Shanghai 21 Culture Promotion Co., Ltd.
中國會 The China Club
香港文學出版社有限公司 The Hong Kong Literary Press Co. Limited
斑馬谷文化發展 (北京) 有限公司 Zebra Valley Culture Development

Printed in Hong Kong